Tonight the Summer's Over

RORY WATERMAN was born in Belfast in 1981, but grew up mostly in rural Lincolnshire. He has degrees from Durham University and the University of Leicester, and completed a PhD in 2012 whilst living in Bristol. He is currently Lecturer in English and Creative Writing at Nottingham Trent University, co-edits the magazine *New Walk*, and writes critical prose for various publications. This is his first collection of poetry.

T0099112

RORY WATERMAN

Tonight the Summer's Over

CARCANET

Acknowledgements

Acknowledgements are due to the editors of the following publications, in which many of these poems first appeared, sometimes in slightly different forms: *Able Muse, Agenda, The Best British Poetry 2012* (Salt, 2012), *The Bow-Wow Shop, Clinic, The Dark Horse, Days of Roses Anthology II, Endymion, English, The Interpreter's House, Manchester Review, The Morning Star, The New Criterion, New Poetries V* (Carcanet, 2011), *The North, Not Only the Dark* (WordAid, 2011), *Obsessed with Pipework, Orbis, PN Review, Poetry, Poetry Review, Raintown Review, Shit Creek Review, Smiths Knoll, Stand, Staple, The Times Literary Supplement.*

I am grateful for the gift of a Hawthornden Fellowship in 2012.

First published in Great Britain in 2013 by
Carcanet Press Limited
Alliance House
Cross Street
Manchester M2 7AQ

www.carcanet.co.uk

A CIP catalogue record for this book is available from the British Library

ISBN 978 1 84777 207 7

The publisher acknowledges financial assistance from Arts Council England

Supported by
**ARTS COUNCIL
ENGLAND**

Typeset by XL Publishing Services, Exmouth

Contents

Navigating

A heron burst from the bank where we hadn't seen it
to out of sight beneath the tree-bitten sky
      the way we were heading.
Let's follow! So, a dawdle became the pursuit
of something that we couldn't realise.

We paddled and ruddered, slick through spilling rapids,
round snags and boulders, churned small dark-skinned deeps
      as otters and crayfish hid;
sparrows and whatnot cheeped; cows chewed at the lip
of a sudden meander, and watched us ignoring them;

and inverted willows shivered with river-weeds,
where toppled half-drowned boughs cut withering chevrons
      along each shadowed straight.
We were happy – weren't we? – because each bend was blind.

We must pursue, and not expect to find.

Family Business

The boatman stares through million-pock-marked waters,
tapping a cigarette, shying from the rain
in mac and wellies, beneath a London plane
that rustles and drips. He turns and tells his daughter
to bolt the hut. Tonight the summer's over.
He heaves the skiff to the boatshed, ties the lines
and double-locks the door. She fits a sign:
CLOSED FOR SEESON. They load a battered Land Rover
with cash tin, radio, stools, as fast as they can,
for it's raining harder. Lightning blanks the dark,
and then they're away, the wiper thwacking its arc.
She glances at this ordinary man
then shuts her eyes: she's damp and tired and bored.
He drives more gently. Neither says a word.

Visiting Grandpa

He gave her a photo of great-grandma Alice
and a small box of medals he'd won in the War.
She tried on his glasses and giggled, and listened
to the clicks of his pacemaker, cheek to chest,
and wound up his watch, and shook-shook his tablets,
but he didn't say what they were for.

When he died of the cancer she wasn't to see him,
her mum said. You can't show a child of four
what the body might do to itself. So one evening
she learned about heaven, how people looked down
and smiled. And she tried not to cry, and she hid
the medals her grandpa once wore.

Retrospect

How does an owl get hit by a train?
Pristine, unbloodied, slightly flat:
at thirteen you don't think it's anything
you won't see the same way again

like toys, cartoons, just months ago.
It's stiff as board, you find. You fan a wing
which springs half back towards its holding.
You lift it by a talon to show

your mates you're not afraid. Four frail claws curl
in your cruel hand – you're holding hands
with a wise dead owl, and learning something
inscrutable you still can't understand.

What Passing Bells

A policeman blocks the road so I stop
and tut and tap the wheel and find a sweet
and scrape it through its wrapper with my teeth.
More cars stop. Then bright rustling up the street
from snare drums and some reedy trumpet-calls
remind us all what day it is. In front

the noise grows to a wail. The band files past,
the soldiers, local groups, then ranks of kids
half out of time, with backs and shoulders stiff,
some looking at us looking at them for
just long enough to say a thousand words
in glares. They don't remember any wars

but TV ones, and nor (confess) do you:
just TV wars, most justice-compromised
in barren lands, for rich commodities
I'm using up, a quiet friend by my side
with best intentions, clothes from Oxfam shops,
our flask packed for a cold stroll by the sea.

Rebirth Island

The longed-for dash of waves is heard, and wide
His luminous home of waters opens, bright
And tranquil, from whose floor the new-bathed stars
Emerge, and shine upon the Aral Sea.
                    Matthew Arnold, *Sohrab and Rustum*

The world's fourth largest lake. On a tiny island
shaped like a battered crown, they primed for war
with Petri dishes of anthrax, bubonic plague,
brucellosis, smallpox, tularemia.
Monkeys and mice were infected and dissected
in labs set back from corridors set back
from longer corridors, where lights were bright
and on all night. And beyond the guarded doors
the air washed clean and cold, smelled softly of fish.

But the Aral was silting. There were other needs,
and rivers that pumped the lake were bled away
to burgeoning places, to flourish as cotton fields.
So the mainland thrust for the island across new flats,
littered with lopsided hulls; the lakeside towns
fell many miles from shore; then the climate changed

in far-off Moscow, the microbiologists went
from Rebirth to newer things, and the site decayed
in silence and wind. And soon it was de-islanded,
repatriated, shored by a shrubbed, salted plateau.

And in Moynaq, in Aralsk, some stayed and wanted to go.

In the Avenue of Limes

A dribbling afternoon
in Gloucestershire. Through
the National Arboretum,
between broad name-tagged trees,
we squelched in half-blue gloom.

Not like your New England:
postcard reds and ochres
reflected in chill lakes,
drowning the shivered stems
of whitened spires. No: a glum
and quiet way to age,
pallid in a damp-thick
whinny of breezing rain.
Guessing a quick route back

towards the car, we cut
across the regal, bristling
'Avenue of Limes'
where autumn was falling
in ceaseless drifts of twos
and fours from a quiver
of frail mottled canopy
to clotting mottled ground
where I lost myself in you

dashing to clutch at flurries
of washed-out hearts. Dashing
to clutch at flurries of washed-
out hearts. Dashing to clutch
at flurries of washed-out hearts.

An Email from Your Mother

Moses won't eat. The kitten a girl brought back
to save from the bag will die without her there
two decades later. You slacken in despair,
griming my shoulder. For something else will die

with Moses. Home will never, quite, be waiting
the way it was; your childhood is receding
too far. Is growing older, then, forced unclenching?
Does my arm curl round you like weed?

Two

The toddler with fat red cheeks in a blue Babygro,
legs skew-whiff, blond hair in a motherly clump,
face trapped in cute consternation, lets me know
through widened eyes that what happens to him matters.

The floppy-eared teddy he clutches in that studio
is a prop, not a gift. He doesn't realise
yet, but soon he'll have to let it go.
He hugs it because he's told to, looking up at the camera,

at the trap of a violent flash-bulb exploding. So
thirty-year-younger eyes stare blind at their future.

Growing Pains

1 DISTANCE

Mummy goes to court and Daddy goes
to court, poppet, and in there they sort out
what happens next, love – where you go to bed
and go to school. That's all this is about.

      And who deserves you most? Who's the best
      at cuddling you and saying never mind
      each time you piss the bed? It's like a test
      and you're the prize, my sweet. The experts know,

they've done their sums and read their clever books.
That judge man, he's a clever clever man.
So be a big boy, kid, and dry your eyes.
We all love you. We're doing all we can.

And now – my word! – you're twenty-five years older,
pulling affidavits from a folder.

2 FOR MY FATHER

...discord which has ripped
you from your father, stripped
away known places, play and friends...
             Andrew Waterman, 'For My Son'

So I grew up a 'case', in Lincolnshire,
'abducted', as you'd have it, just turned two,
when 'she revoked [my] birthright'/ brought me here.
This is my tale of 'access times' with you.

Daddy came each month. On Saturday
the social worker's car would take me down
to the Lindum Guesthouse, seven miles away
in Lincoln, then we'd hug and walk around

the shops, and up the hill to Castle Square –
a gape-mouthed gatehouse one way, and the other
the honeyed Minster penetrating air.
And, in another world, my loving mother.

For this was Daddy's place. You taught me how
the Normans built those arches, how that well
gave Romans all their water from the brow
of this glacial hill, beneath which Celts

came sliding in small boats to Brayford Pool,
where Vikings later came to overhaul
and settled with the natives. At my school
we hadn't 'done' this yet, us boys and girls

all learning to fit in, and here I stood
in my home town and breaking it apart
with Irish Daddy, near to whom I slept.
Then Sunday would arrive and I'd depart

full of stories, tears, cake, love, resentment,
our candle burning brightly to a stub
in Lincoln Minster, seven miles away,
as I got home and you got to the pub.

A swift one for your long hard journey home.
And though I didn't love one of you more
the cries and bedtime hugs with Mum at home
were urgent, but it's you whom I cried *for*.

And that was most of it. Remember how
I'd speak into the Dictaphone? 'Explain'
my feelings on where I'd 'like to live now',
in a town I'd only heard of, called Coleraine,

whilst sitting in the Lindum, downing sweets?
At two I'd not grown used to anywhere.
By five the squat stone houses, leafy streets
of Dunston, rural Lincolnshire was where

my life was, if for better or for worse.
The court heard our recording and agreed.
And Lincoln was a blessing and a curse,
where Daddy lived each month, and lived with me.

3   IRELAND, 10

'This is your homeland.' Looking at
a row of mountains for the first
time in living memory –
that child of sunken Lincolnshire,
           of flattened vowels and reticence –
           I knew that it was not. And why
           he wanted it to be.

Those Ireland shirts he'd put me in
on access visits! Toddling round
a chipped bust of King George III
in Lincoln Castle, sporting green,
        had fractured me. The first house that
        I'd known, where he still lived, and drank,
        no more to me than photographs

until that week. But always my
'other home'. The leafy bank
I'd dreamed was there, behind that lens,
thick and wild with gooseberries
        and blackberries, rosehips and thorns,
        like Mum had, was a breezeblock school
        for Catholic kids with uniforms

and habits that I didn't know,
accents, odd names, ginger hair,
school holidays at funny times.
I'd watch them through the window, there.
        Then back at school and flooded with
        a slurry of ineptitudes
        I'd brag about that 'other home'

and 'other me' – not *here*, like *them* –
the Irish me that never was,
the bronze-haired friends I never made,
the mansion where Dad never lived.
        And mourned the loss of all these things
        I'd never had and always had;
        and grew, estranged from Lincolnshire
        and desperate to get out of there.

Access Visit

Your afternoon pint; my Britvic pineapple juice;
a bag of prawn cocktail gaping in the middle.
The lounge at the Wig & Mitre was Daddy's choice.
And then, at six, my taxi home; a cuddle
before I left you waving at the corner,
bound for my mother, our monthly weekend over.
And she would always seem a little warmer
than when I'd left, and I'd be slightly colder.

How could I know what an alcoholic was?
The Wig & Mitre's now Widow Cullen's Well.
The snugs have been pulled out, the walls made bare;
but the place still has the same sweet, musty smell,
and I'm going in for a drink again because
I know I'll find a part of us in there.

Seeing Him Off at the Station

A stump clasps the tarmac, its twisted roots taut
like an old man's hand, though the wrist is cut clean.
The boughs wait in piles, cubed and saw-dusted; but
the stump won't let go, thrusts out crowns of fresh shoots.

She sits on it, staring at rails. He's gone home
to the other woman – humming in their kitchen –
whose bedtime kiss will be different, though she won't know it.
A speck turns a bend, turns to train, fizzes in, wheezes on.

Craigmillar Castle at Dusk

Whatever else we are, we're foreign up here.
The trinkets back in the ticket office say
Scottish and Proud and out along the bay
a line of chimneys smudge the clouds,
these gusts and hundred gulls are harsh and loud,
those batteries of tower-blocks dull and sheer.

The dovecote that fed Queen Mary. Bolted and barred.
Pigeons scatter-bomb the chamber walls,
blink in unmeant crannies, shuffle, call
and flutter across us, through sighing windows.
We avoid them. As the last light goes, we go.

A flagless flagpole rattles towards the stars.

Faroe Islands: Notes for Three Photographs

i.

Arctic terns head-butt spume
then flick away, beak-heavy
in lithe, bounding *vs*,
or work the same strip
of wind-whorled saltwater
time and time over;

each whip and dip of wing
as normal, as novel
as the carcass I saw
basking on rocks at Húsar,
neck jack-knifed, black crest shining,
guts and sockets alive.

ii.

I ate puffins at Viðareiði,
a cliff-side-net-snatched delicacy,
with shallots, mangetouts,
a saucière of thick puffin gravy,
ridiculous under
fat silver cutlery.

I sucked each tiny bone, left
a splat-doused tablecloth, felt
a bit more interesting. Endless
grey patterns slid before island
a mile from the window.
Juts of cliff looked empty.

iii.

Echoless loneliness
in glowing mist
on the cliff-top at Enniberg.
Just kittiwakes here,
some tacking through breeze, feet curled,
more chattering in alcoves.

My wife slices cheese
onto bread in her lap,
feet splayed like a child's,
as I sit on the rim,
stare through milk,
push at death with my boots.

Nettles

I go to harvest nettles in the wood
with vaguest thoughts of soups and stews and teas,
and wade through stems that break

across my knees, not thinking of the wreck
my steps have made, remembering my Nan
using an afternoon to gouge and twist
her shadow with a spade

for rhubarb that we never ate,
for pies we never made.

Reverdie

The broadened buzzard
glides in an orbit,
as if on a wire,
then twists, breaking free;

a bee revs its engine
and limps from stamen
to stamen, then lifts,
chicanes to the trees.

Your gaze follows one,
mine the other;
they mingle silently
in the thickening canopy.

Seeing Baby Emrys in Gwynedd

for Emrys Jackson

The distant rained-on pines mist under crags –
thin squibs of forest smoke that slow the pulse.
The lopping tide has turned up jellyfish, dulse
and flints of wood, and netting, bottles, bags,

so what at first seemed mystical also seems
pulverised by what we've turned it to.
What do you make of it? Like fruit, your dreams
are silently forming. You do what babies do:

gape, squeal, dribble, vomit, suck your toes.
Life is going as planned, we'd all agree.
A month since last time, and you've forgotten me,
it feels. But we'll get there. Mind how you go.

Salisbury, After the Argument

Though svelte, the spire falls stupidly short
of the firmament, stands solid against
the sheets of wet we hide from under
a lime, and tinkles the hour through rips
of thunder, its pinnacle glowing the more
for dying light.
              We eyeball it
through swashing branches, that crafted tip,
determined to make all right. We fall
stupidly short. We brush the firmament.

For R.S. Thomas

This wealth is for the few
And chosen. Those who crowd
A small window dirty it
With their breathing...
                    R.S. Thomas, 'The Small Window'

Bird's Rock. Craig yr Aderyn in a tongue
I care for but don't speak, and never will.
The back slopes off like any other hill;
the front's a forehead of cliff. Choughs feed their young
and judder through the moaning wind below
our feet. She squeezes my hand and pulls me back.
Down there, a tractor totters up a track.
We lob our apple-cores. No one could know
we're on this bluff. You wouldn't like it, would you?
You wouldn't want us dirtying the view.

Coming Home

My mother kept me informed:
a sad, warm, phone-grained voice
enticed me home, for once –
could not prepare me for

the dying old dog by the door
whose too-big leather collar
gives name and number,
to carry her back unharmed.

From a Birmingham Council Flat

The usual wash of post by the door:
bills and statements, a couple of Christmas cards
in June. Neighbours thought they'd not seen John
for months, then could take the flies no more
and someone wondered where they'd all come from
and called us in. The stench was hot and hard,
my stomach hit my throat. Forensics packed
him up and took him off. We cleaned the floor

of ash from his last cigarette, and saw
the hollow in the sofa where he stopped
in front of his TV, beneath his lamp,
and fumigated to wipe out the raw
taste of him, between framed photographs
of dimpled schoolchildren. And no one cried
at the sight of the wedding album or patches of damp,
or wondered what he'd bothered living for.

Broadland

Only Bill's boatyard was renting; the others were close-shuttered
but a necklace of bobbing day launches flanked both sides of one pier.

The season was ending and so were we. We were over,
though habit pulled us near, on the grebe-sprinkled water,

where swans tucked their heads in behind, nudging up to the rushes,
and made do for the words we couldn't know we would utter.

Where Were You When...

...those girders gave? There were signs we cared:
reams of sympathy, uncertainty;
relentless shots of figures treading air;
wreaths and crosses; services; silences.

We knew it meant that thousands more would die.
Of course. Some said they'd once been in that Square
between them both, and watched illusive sky
overbalance concrete, over there.

In Lincoln, in respect, a few things shut.
Daily, the Minster's tower cut the ground
with shifting shadow, like a huge sundial
no one could read, and pushed the baskers round.

The Outings

I remember when this were covered in sheep
he said, his head full of meadow, his eyes on a car park/
supermarket/petrol station combo.
They hate it but it's cheap. Through the door-wheel they go.

Christmas is being made to last at the wrong end.
Past the frontline of pyramids of special biscuits
an obstruction of toys: they could kit themselves out
with pool table, ping-pong table, table-football table

but they're here for dad's big shop. And life now is split
into fortnights by afternoons like this.
And they're glad that nothing changes quite enough
to make them talk about it.

These hours are so familiar: the bleeping scanners;
the browsing at islands of cheese, at the reeking fish counter;
the quiet alleys of kitchenware; the reaching for tins;
the dozens and dozens of roasting chickens,

legs crossed on the spit, cartwheeling endlessly
in what seems like bliss; the cards and wrap
by the exit, all full of snow. And back through the doors
the feathery car-park trees, still more green than yellow.

A Suicide

Away. And for a moment as you tipped,
traversed the awful point of no return
and yelled, stretch-torsoed in the faraway,

you faced us. Eyes unseeing mirrored mine:
I thought of me; the you in me, in us;
and all the things you'd given us to say.

West Summerdale Ave

The sprinkler slashes its crest across your lawn
and back again, and slashes its crest across
and back again, and slashes its crest across....
Your cat, beyond it, knits the air and yawns
a dislocated yawn, and from the tree
the nesting-box flobs out a fluttering wren.
We hear the ice-cream van come round again
and over the road a clown returns from a party.

Suburban American houses aren't built to last.
Wall-panels fell each time the digger struck
and soon the plot was a square of treacled muck.
What it had meant was buried in the past,
was laid to rest, by being turned to air.
And now a newer home is standing there.

53° 09'33.17" N, 0° 25'33.18" W

A lodge-house to an estate, once: the front wall
still ends with one redundant brick gatepost,
its rustic latch clicking only to wind,
and the clean bulk of its limestone cap
shorn of clogs of English ivy, carious and precarious.

There used to be a long metal water-butt
out of bounds, snug to a wall, pungent
with moss and webs, its content a black
lilting mirror when I'd raise the lid
that was wooden and rotten and gave slightly.

And there was a low-slung roof on a breezeblock annexe
with a fat windowsill and convenient external piping
that occasionally broke and had to be mended;
and a cigar-box of old green pennies and shards of pot
from the garden, out of sight in a cracked soffit.

But the side gate remains, a wrought iron cross-hatch
mass-produced in a distant foundry, showing
bends for the feet that are no longer mine,
that kicked off and made it a shrill, dull swing;
and the fence is the matt-green my grandmother painted,
though tarnished now, and in places peeling.

To Help the Birds through Winter

i.m. D.A. Eagle (1917–1997)

She knots our turkey carcass to the yew
with garden twine, and leaves it jigging
and twirling with the wind. There's work to do

and here she is at the kitchen window.
Her heart is giving out. Her serous eyes
are failing, too. And before I go

to Spain with school, in five months' time,
she will not tell me what I know.
And I'll not ring. And grimed, frayed string
will be flitting on its branch, like torn rigging.

The Lake

Mid-May now, and the hawthorns have started
foaming and stinking. They glow under clear night sky.
The car park is empty, the vending hatches shut.
When I was too small to stand somebody left
a girl near here to die, unconscious, full of come,
and gagged, in case. Flopped her in the silt
with care. The moon flutters a meaningless smile
and on the surface it skits everywhere.

Shrine for a Young Soldier, Castle Drogo

Easy to pick out, Gioconda-faced:
here he crouches in Oxford sepia-blue;
here in the Eton Boys' XI;
here in a family portrait, in casuals;

here in straitening khaki, moustached like a man,
clutching a bayonet proudly: Major Drewe.
'With the Angels in Heaven'.

The day the letter arrived from the Front
the butler stood silent behind the door;
the maids waited, eyes blank, and prayed for their masters
in their cluttered living room, newspapers spread with the War.

The golden child rancid in mud
and horror brought home like a catkill left
on a worn-through scullery floor.

On Derry City Walls, 1992

I was ten. I might still take Dad's arm
now and then. Where the Bogside sprawls to green hills
he'd nod at what half-blindness meant he'd not see,
say: *The border runs right between us and those farms.*

Then he'd point down at Free Derry Corner, the Inn,
the murals of gasmasks and thirteen men dead.
His outrage was weighted. I washed in it, like love.
Then at his house at night, before bed,

we'd crank up the 'Irish songs': 'Boolavogue',
'Dirty Old Town', 'Skibbereen', 'Spancil Hill'.
I'm full of them still. They were solder between
us Mum couldn't use, that sustained me back home.

But, like 'Dirty Old Town' evokes Salford, Lancs,
my voice was pure Lincoln. Homogeneous Lincoln
was not where I came from, I knew, as I prayed
for my best friend's dad, still in the Gulf, in a tank.

Unfolding

You did some cuts and shook it out and there it was:
a chain of figures holding hands and touching feet.
Daddy got down the crayons

and so you blotted it in with scrawling lines and swirls
in purple, green, black, blue, and put on faces
and looked at it and saw that it was very good
and wrote your name on it

and Mummy said that she thought it was very good
and stuck it on the fridge with Blu-tack. Sixteen years
blinked by. It stayed there creasing, spattered, half-ignored,
yellowing and being covered up with postcards,
and went in a tin

when Mum and Dad did the kitchen up, when you
had graduated, got a job, and they had time
and money to spare, retirement plans. And four months after
you hit that sycamore, struck half your brain away,
they took it in to you, asked do you remember this?
But you didn't say.

Marstrand

The juts of island with a fortress where
Sweden tried out solitary confinement
for five cold years, and one victim went strange
and chiselled his fingers to putrid stumps
in the window stone.

                    A great cormorant
on a boulder, staring through itself
at fleeting, darting shoals of silver-black,
stirs, slaps the inlet to shudders
and rises in steady flight.

Winter Morning, Connecticut

Your parents' house. Your bedroom full of books
and photo albums. Clothes you won't throw out.
The Hepburn calendar, a decade old,
silted, faded, skewered to a wall.
The bed you might have shared with other men
when they were boys, the bed that went with you
to university.

We leave it, drink hot coffee, bundle up
and step out on a lawn of blazing snow,
shedding lines of prints that drift apart
and back together, let our stumbles show
and find us huddled here
with soft bright pellets scattered through our hair
as though embroidered there.

A Wedding Photograph

for my parents

At my sun/rain/wind-flushed wedding that November
neither of them knew they both had cancer.
Divorce, a custody war, some twenty-four years;

a happiness had thrust them back together,
had made them seem a pair –
not sickness, or despair.

No endless yestertalk or choking tears,
none of that stuff. But quietly, alone,
we all remember:

I think, now, how I might have hooked your arms
for our photo between those gust-trembled puddles,
the patterns breaking, scattering, regathered.

Back in the Village

1

Where did that child go, straying down the lanes
in thinning snow, seeing footsteps turn
to slush then rain, one cold eventless day;

or clambering through the ruined manor house,
all done up now, worn-in and trellis-guarded?
He knows their cellars and lofts better than they
do still, I'm sure. Where is that child today?

He's outside what was Paul's house, with his wife,
in silent night beneath crisp constellations –
star-swarms and nests of secret nebulae –
the car on gravel by the village pub.
He's walking round The Green, where once he played

throwball – that's a game his mates invented,
dependent on a tree that's been removed.
New children wouldn't know that one had stood there
and wouldn't give a tuppence anyway.

He's leaning on the sign by his old school:
new roof, new teaching staff, much else the same;
kids home asleep (tomorrow is a school day).

He's nothing to them; all of this is theirs.
He's handed down the torch, though, in a way.

2

Why would that old boy watch us on the field
at break-time, over the gate that's now a fence?
Pip the Jack Russell tight to his ankle
and paper in hand, that was Mr Arndale,
with fingers like tubers, drab cap, wry face
and stories to match, and humbugs to keep us from football
a moment longer. A bungalow is for sale
on Middle Street: the gnomes, the stepping stones
have gone from his tiny plot, where weak tall nettles
tremble in cauling rainfall, and a nest
of deflated sacking couches a dark pool of runoff
by what's become of his potting shed, greening, rotting.
And we were his prototypes, his certainty
of life still growing whole. The ghost of him is me.

Compulsions

'She'd call police, social services; I was confused,
an only angry boy. It's no excuse.
She called my uncle, who threatened to beat me up
and over he drove. And I had had enough
and cycled to town, avoiding the bigger roads
in case I was seen, and hid behind a payphone
until, around 2 a.m., a policeman came
and drove me home. It must sound like a game
of cat and mouse, a tactical exchange;
for a year or so it was normal – my "coming of age"
when the small foul egg of resentment gave birth to a crack
and I smashed our faces in it until we were sick.'
Recall what you said, as we ambled round the park:
'It must be a great inspiration for your work.'
How I shuddered. But now I must confess
that's what this poem embodies, more or less.

The Fields over Winceby Battlefield

Sown every year, mown and churned every year.
Each January now, machine-sliced loaves of muck
clutter the acres across this jigsaw of cropland,
dour and mute. In March the shoots, the hares,
gunshots and starlings bursting from the holts;
then late spring with its height, downpours, dried snails.

Over the overgrown hedge at the edge
a hamlet huddles beside a hay-barn;
a kestrel stuns its world and a speck glitters
where solar panels shield a low bungalow.
The rape's broken out, smearing the fields with butter.
The earth doesn't know what it's known.

Spring Shower, Metheringham Fen

We watched the storm drift in across the Fen,
swallowing farms, flushing out blue,
dragging wheezing gusts of oily rain
that slalomed down the windowpane
and pattered millionfold across the wheat.

Ants filed through the cracks in grouting
jostling like potatoes in a chute.
The window whinnied. Half a mile
beyond the barn, an artic' slamming through spray
flicked on its headlights, went on its way.

We saw the storm slide through and out again.
A chirrup burst from the sycamore,
earthworms glinted like morsels on the tar
and sunshine drew us through the door
to cold, sweet air and puddles full of sky.

The Beck

– Because we loved the beck. I tread the reeds
then up to the hump of the bridge, cradling the urn
like a nursed fledgling, and lean on the rail
to let you out. My face and hands wobble earnestly.
The devouring mirror takes you in in silence.

Keepsakes

Chairs and *chaises longues* arranged for sitting in,
with teasels in their hollows; china cups
on gate-leg tables, with tortoiseshell snuff boxes,
Bakelite telephones and Toby jugs,
some chipped with web-cracked noses; dull mirrors that warp
the roomful as I pass them, or fatten my legs;
a photo of a soldier from the War,
oak-framed, mouthing something, buttons white
with sun-fading and Brasso, marked as 'Scuffed';
the constellation of brass companion sets
taking up a corner at the back;
the bawdy cards and hunting prints and pastels
marked 'LINCOLN MINSTER', and flocks of shimmering Spitfires
whirring up through bold faux-Whistler skies
in stark formations, on to Victory
in masses of blues and whites and tangerines.

More pictures than wall, more bric-a-brac than floor.
A century and some of neglect, of cleared-out houses,
of looked-after-then-left. Old trades and whims
offered up in clusters round a hall,
away from wet and rot, not allowed to be junk,
whatever once they meant. Vague familial
discarded worlds that died and hide in us.
And that is what my mother comes here for.
So now we're back in Horncastle again,
for a day under buzzing strip-lights in cold rooms
and frogmarching a cabinet to the car,
a Victorian planter, Edwardian wine tables,
for her to look at sometimes, bring out for guests;
long hours of agreeing things are nice,
half-bored, slow-stepping round tat.
But cherishing it, a little bit, perhaps.

'You're a shower of bastards'

But how shall man's, or manner's, form appear,
Which while I write, do change from what they were?

Thomas Bastard

Yes: we were clean. And sure: collectives
might, sometimes, be more objective
about what things do or the company they keep:
a randiness of rabbits, a shit of sheep,

a wad of bankers, a dirge of teachers,
a ponder-and-pretence of preachers,
a heartache of liberals, a blindfold of Tories,
a goredom of Chuck Palahniuk stories.

Well, after all, jellyfish come in a smack,
flamingos in a stand and hounds in a pack;
there's a cloud of gnats and a cloud of bats,
a shrewdness of apes and a glaring of cats.

But I'm not quite sure what a hit-and-run father
has to do with soap and lather.
We might have scrubbed and splashed on Brut,
but we have finer attributes.

Note to Self:
Chip Shop Battered Sausage and Other Meat

Though I know it's full of shit
I cram it in,
savour grease-swill with my tongue,

prod fat-damp batter detritus
with spit-slimed stumps,
and hoist to bird-like upturned open face.

I've seen boys flexing pecs
in dwarfing mirrors –
been one, almost: sought advice on 'loading'

from a brute on a twenty-
egg-white diet;
bit lip through curls, each muscle-altering.

I'll take an island. Fat, alone, I'll sit
cross-legged outside
my tent, shelling winkles,

the radio half-hissing
football results.
Scanning sea, sand-footed, thinning

to essence.

Stopping for a Moment on Exmoor

An eye-shifting gunburst of warbles!
A flush of starlike trembles
then instant space,
a bobbing twig-branch;

and the trill of a distant wife,
hands-on-hips, compelling me on,
reclaiming me into her life.

Back

for Rachel Chambers

So – as I argued about the prices of laptops,
worried about not doing any work
and cleared the desk, made pots of tea for two,
picnicked near Brecon – you huddled up a gorge
in Ladakh, as flash floods thundered away
five of your companions, slower to run,
so drowned behind you. And I've no right to say

what this is like. I'm silent, nod, half-smile.
You speak so calmly: of digging with your hands
to tunnel in; that constant smash of water;
dodging rock-fall, 'like a computer game';
four comfortless nights with death, wanting your mum.
But jetlagged tonight, between my wife and me,

you sipped our gin, dropped earrings down a chair,
destroyed a glass, spilled bags across the floor,
your same dishevelled self. And how you survived
is a mystery to us, we cannot joke.
Nor dare we think why perhaps we love you more.
And now we've gone to bed. My note reads just:

'It's good to have you back.' Words can fail.
But such things, Rachel, are coal for poetry,
so here we are. Because there *you* are now
in the next-door room, curled up on the sofa
yet again, my friend. It's old, but plush, and deep,
and holds you like a seed squat in a palm
as rain jitters down the window while you sleep.

Infant

You scrabbled into sterile air
with stubby fingers, pudgy feet,
and burst with toothless cries
to tell us you were there.

And fistulas that shouldn't be
were widening. You could not know
your parents and theirs needed you,
stood by, and watched you go.

Stranger

Snot-billed brats in playsuits lump about
in ball-pens, squiggle through tubes
to squishy mats, then laugh or scream again.
Others chew biscuits, or writhe like dogs in prams.

Enough to put me off my carrot *pressé*,
my hunk of crumble cake. Then a two-foot scruff
with saucer eyes waddles to my knee,

fingers his nose as if uncorking it,
and asks me plainly, sweetly, who I am.

Perhaps I'm not the man I'd like to be.

Sendai

Bristol, March 2011

The panning shot, and whine
of helicopter blades.
The houses like untethered boats
in Avonmouth marina.
I followed the thought to its conclusion
and found myself, staring
at a dank Wilmott's whitebeam
three months before it
explodes for the moths
in a lonely thicket.

Fall

'9/11 was worse than the Srebrenica Massacre because it happened in Manhattan.'

A body hit the sea; America hit the sky.
A Good Day became tomorrow, and here you are
in small-town six months later, where the flagpoles
are glinting at the bulb. So what can you answer?

You're the welcomed guest; you got here in their car;
it seems so plausible and everything else so far.

*

The leaves aren't good this year: unseasonal torrents
have old-Englanded New England. You tell someone
what part of England Wales is, for mutual convenience,
and saunter to the porch, swatting bugs

an inch from the rain. The grass smells as it should;
the dark-bleeding tree-bark takes you home again.

*

Not that it always rained. Once more you're shaping
sand by a sun-blanched Barmouth, where Daddy taught you
about Ceaușescu, the orphans of Romania.
You'd eat in that night, and send the savings there.

You're called from the stoop to a table of steak, and prayer:
Keep us safe, dear Jesus, and help the needy everywhere.

Autumn 2011

Hallowed Turf

This ground holds seven thousand but it only fills for derby games.
The green and white is peeling from the signs.
My first name signals something here: the battered main stand
                                                    bears it. I
could follow this club. It never could be mine.

It's match day. Lines of mostly men and boys
click shivering through the gates. A song breaks dutifully through
                                                    them all.
Soon they're in. And faded, where they were,
gapes *FTQ*, quick-pen-stroked like a runic slogan, down the wall.

The Shipwreck Memorial a Mile from Town

is backed by whin, cracked benches, cracked railings, sand.

The wheel freewheeling above the Promenade
is far too far away to hear; its flocks of lights

shift like code. A boy toes the foam at the shore
and whoops as the wavelets fold across his feet;

jet-skis thud in and spin at the mouth of the quay.
And beyond them the nothing sun is falling through nothing,

past this flat and glistening stomach that has no body.

Over the Heath

The truck grinds by
and pumps out grit;
the road glints and
goes still.

The barn owl that
had not finished here
returns. But with
its fill

of scavenges,
face ruffled in mulch,
the vole is lost
and safe

so the silent spectre
flits away, its
moon face to
the moon

and rears unknown
against a copse,
claws tipped for
the strafe

and something dies
too soon.

He filled her between
the hay-bales in
that Dutch barn, now
abandoned,

where the wind
catches its breath
in the stanchions,
air-gun holes.

Then they sprang up
light and lightsome
and she tugged his hand
with her hand

as the breeze pulled
at the poppy-heads
and rabbits shrank
round boles.

But how soon he'd
grow indifferent
as the tick she
couldn't see

that was part of
her for longer
than he would choose
to be.

Out to the Fen

Suddenly, the shattered hedges, ancient copses,
our huge ruined villages, give way as
dimpled fields tilt to the Fen
and the treeless otherworld begins.

A farmer slices a vast parched field to a desert of stalks
in acres of dust and haze. Blueflies thrum
unperturbed, by a verdant ditch straight
as a Midwestern state highway, vanishing both ways

into hardly a ridge: a slope that stretches
and loops for hundreds of miles to the same sea.
Along its lip, behind dykes, the low farms and
hardened cottages stare across the flats.

It's like a coast, but what might be sea
is a sea of overstretched meadows, fresh green wheat
nodding like so many donkeys,
dotted with clumps of poppies,

and the elders have flowered. We snip
the heads by dusk, in a silence of ditch noise
and birdsong, for cordial and fritters,
sometime later, then scatter

hares in the headlamps, and thud through clumps
of skitting gnats as distant lights
blink to let us know buildings are
over there, people are over there, and now

it's time to go.

Boy finds the fulmar, like archaeopteryx,
mashed in rock and splayed awry

so he stubs its beak, smooths its neck,
fingers its empty eye.

Lift the purest feather from the wreck.
Ignore the seagulls laughing against the sky.